COOKING for one

{or even two}

More than 150 recipes

By Dr. Duane Lund

COOKING *for* one
{ or even two }

More than 150 recipes

© Copyright 2012

By Lund S and R Publications, Staples, Minnesota 56479

Except for brief quotations—

First printing 2012

Printed USA, etc.

ISBN-13: 978-0-9740821-8-9
ISBN-10: 0-9740821-8-X

Dedication

To John (Jack) Wilson, a darned good Mayor

of a darned good town, Staples, Minnesota.

This book was Jack's idea.

Table *of* Contents

CHAPTER 1
Breakfasts

Hotcakes (pancakes) 12
Package Mix 13
Pancakes from Scratch 14
Gourmet Cakes..15
Waffles 16
Gourmet French Toast 17
Fried Eggs 18
Boiled Eggs 19
Omelets 20
Individual Omelets....................................21
Ingredients for My Favorite Omelet 22
Scrambled Eggs 23
Poached Eggs 24
Minnesota Skillet Breakfast......................25
Chicken Broth with Eggs 26
Bacon...27
Sausage Patties..28
Pork Links..29
Breakfast Ham..30
Baking Powder Biscuits 31
Blueberry Muffins......................................32
Gourmet Oatmeal......................................33
Cocoa Mix..34

CHAPTER 2
Starters

Apple Slices with Cheese 36
Woodticks on a Popple Tree 37
Deep-fried, Battered
   Morel Mushrooms 37
Stuffed Celery Pieces 38
Dates Stuffed with Cheese
   and Wrapped with Bacon 39
Deep-fried Mushrooms
   with Melted Cheese Dip 40
Eggs Stuffed with Smoked Fish 41
Smoked Fish and Cucumber Spread 42
Smoked Fish-Dill Spread 42
Guacamole Dip..43

Shrimp Dip 43	
Cucumber Dip 44	
Hawaiian Spread 44	
Nutty-Cheese Spread 45	
Marinated Olives 45	
Bruschetta Appetizer #1 46	
Bruschetta Appetizer #2 47	
Bruschetta Appetizer #3 48	
Tomato Salsa 49	
Garden Salsa 50	
Favorite Snack:	
Caramel Corn-Old Dutch Style 51	

CHAPTER 3
Soups

Chilled Tomato Soup 54
Carrot Soup with Apple 55
Fresh Green Pea Soup 56
Garlic and Onion Soup 57
Duck Soup 58
Baked Potato Soup 59
Beer Soup with Pasta and Egg Noodles 60
Creamy Cauliflower Soup 61
Zucchini Soup 62

CHAPTER 4
Salads

Smoked Fish Salad 64
Apple Salad with Bacon 65
Beet Salad 66
Ham and Cheese Salad 67
Beet and Onion Salad 68
Italian Salad 69
Tomato and Cheese Salad 70
Garden Vegetable Salad 71
Pasta Salad with Shrimp 72
Bell Pepper Salad 73
Potato Salad #1 74
Potato Salad with a Touch of Wine 75
Cabbage Salad 76

CHAPTER 5
Sandwiches

Hamburgers 79
Building a Burger 80
Hot Dogs 81
Option #1 81
Option #2 81

Option #3	81
Option #4	81
Option #5	81
Brats	82
Fish Sandwich	82
Mashed Potatoes on Brats	83
Smoked Meat Sandwich	84
Tomato-Cheese Sandwich	85
Open-face Egg Sandwich	86
Herring and Potato Sandwich	87
Ham Sandwich	87
Flaked Fish Sandwich	88
BLT	88
Grilled Spicy Chicken on a Bun	89
Toasted Club Sandwich	90
Lunch Meat Sandwich	91
Apple Club Sandwich	91

CHAPTER 6
Side Dishes

Zucchini with Wine	94
More Zucchini	95
Dandelion Greens	96
Fried Green Tomatoes	97
Summer Vegetable Side Dish	98
Squash Side Dish	99
Red Cabbage Side Dish	100
Mashed Potatoes with Blue Cheese	101
Mashed Potatoes and Browned Onions	102
German Hot Cabbage	103
Fried Potatoes	104
Zesty Corn on the Cob	105
Fried Potatoes with Bacon Bits	106
Rose Germann's Baseball Dumplings	107
Sauce for Your Steak	108

CHAPTER 7
Main Dishes

Baked Freshwater Fish Fillets with Tomato Sauce	110
Pasta with Shrimp	111
Mashed Potatoes with Cream Cheese and Herbs	112
Spicy Spuds	113
Seasoned Potatoes	114
Potato with Herbs on the Grill	115

Cheese-coated Panfish	116
Fillets in Beer Batter	117
Doctoring Your Favorite Beer Batter Recipe	118
Baked Panfish with Parsley and Dill	119
Sauerbraten	120
Cube Steak with Caramelized Onions	121
Potato Pancakes with Apple	122
Doctored Sauerkraut #1	123
Doctored Sauerkraut #2	124
Sauerkraut and Wiener Casserole	125
Beef Stroganoff (German-style)	126
Potato Pancakes	127
Potato Dumplings	128
Pork Chop with Wine Sauce	129
Pasta with Leftover Ham	130
Spaghetti with Meat Sauce	131
Spaghetti with Anchovies	132
Chicken and Pasta Casserole	133
Chicken Thigh Pasta	134
Pasta with Mushroom Sauce	135
Spaghetti with Bacon and Eggs	136
Spaghetti Sauce with Bacon	137
Pasta Sauce without Meat	138
Tortellini with Nuts	139
Fettuccine Alfredo	140
Leftover Chicken Cacciatore	141
Lunch from the Garden	142
Pork Steak with Wine Sauce	143
Sausage-Bean Dinner	144
Italian Sausage Chunks with Vegetables	145
Fettuccine with Bacon Bits	146
Baked Fish with Tomatoes	147
Cheesy Perch	148
Fish Patties	149
Salmon Patties for Two	150
Macaroni and Cheese for Two	151

CHAPTER 8
Desserts

Strawberry Rhubarb Dessert	154
Sauce Made from Dried Fruit	155
Pineapple-Peach Salsa	156
Cherry Salsa	156
Rice Pudding	157
Wild Rice with Wild Berries	157
Orange-Cranberry Bars	158
The Perfect Dessert for Salmon	159

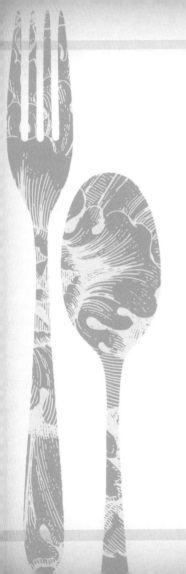

CHAPTER 1
Breakfasts

Hotcakes (Pancakes)

A few tips to guarantee success—for one or for two:

- For richer, more attractive-looking cakes, add one more egg beyond what is called for in the recipe on the package.

- You will have to learn the right consistency through experience, but beware of heavy batter— the cakes will be too think and may not get done in the center. Strive for thin, light cakes about 1/3 inch thick.

- Use a hot griddle, lightly greased. Drops of water will "dance" on the surface when it is ready.

- Makes cakes about 4 to 6 inches in diameter. Never make large pancakes; they tend to be tough on the outside and raw in the center.

- Turn the cakes when bubbles appear in the batter.

- Turn the cakes only once to avoid making them tough.

Package Mix

Cakes prepared from scratch are best, but most mixes on the market today are very good and are more convenient.

Prepare the batter by following the directions on the package. Most package recipes call for the addition of milk, eggs, and a small amount of cooking oil. Powdered milk (mixed with water, of course) is an equal substitute for the liquid variety.

Just observe the tips just mentioned as you prepare the cakes.

Pancakes from Scratch

Ingredients to serve one—double the amounts to serve two:

- ½ cup flour
- ½ cup milk
- 1 T baking powder
- 1 egg (beaten)
- 2 T melted butter
- Dash of salt

Sift all dry ingredients into a bowl. Add egg (already beaten) to milk and mix thoroughly. Add the milk-egg mixture to the dry ingredients, stirring as you add. Continue stirring until relatively smooth, but don't worry about the lumps. Add melted butter and fry on a hot griddle.

Gourmet Cakes

Use any of the previous recipes and simply do one or more (or all) of the following:

- Add fruit, such as blueberries, to the batter.

- Add pre-fried, small pieces of bacon.

- Serve with hot syrup. Always remove the cap before heating! Place the syrup bottle in a pan of hot water. Never heat any container (can, plastic, or glass) without first removing the cover or at least puncturing the top. It will prevent an explosion!

Waffles

Use any of the afore-mentioned pancake recipes, but make the batter a little heavier than for pancakes.

For a richer batter, substitute light cream for the milk.

Preheat the waffle iron until it is steaming hot. Grease the iron lightly (both surfaces) with cooking oil, butter, or margarine to prevent sticking.

Pour on the batter, not quite covering the entire surface; it will expand. Let stand about 30 seconds before closing the lid.

When the iron stops steaming it will be done. Peek cautiously to be sure!

Serve with plenty of butter or margarine and warm syrup.

Gourmet French Toast

Ingredients to serve one—double the amounts to serve two:

1 slice white bread (about ¾ inch thick)
½ cup water or milk
1 T sugar
¼ t salt
1 egg

Beat the egg, water (or milk), sugar, and salt until thoroughly blended. Arrange the thick bread slice in a cake pan. Pour the egg mixture over the bread, turning to coat evenly. Refrigerate, covered, overnight.

In the morning, fry the toast on a well-greased griddle (or in a frying pan) until brown on both sides. This takes about four minutes per side. Use cooking oil, butter, or margarine.

Sprinkle lightly with powdered sugar and/or cinnamon and serve with hot syrup.

Warning! You'll be spoiled for life and will probably never again enjoy French toast in a restaurant!

Fried Eggs

Eggs are probably the most popular of all breakfast foods and they are quick and easy to prepare.

When frying eggs, use a pan with a non-stick surface, like Teflon; otherwise, fry them in oil, butter, or margarine. Bacon grease is another alternative; it may not be healthy, but it adds that bacon flavor to the eggs.

If you use a cover, the eggs will be self-basting. When they are nearly done, a few drops of water on each yolk will "close the eyes" and the steam will help cook the eggs and make them more fluffy.

When using oil or butter, spoon the grease over the eggs two or three times while frying.

For "over easy" turn them gently—so as not to break the yolk—and leave them just long enough to sear-in the yolk. For those who like them "hard fried," just leave them a little longer, remembering that if the eggs are left too long they will get "rubbery."

Add a light dash of salt and pepper before the eggs leave the pan; let others add more if they wish according to individual tastes. Make hot sauce available.

Boiled Eggs

Place the eggs in any convenient container and cover them with water. Bring the water to a boil. Remove the pan from the stove. As a rule of thumb, soft-boiled eggs take another two or three minutes to cook after the pan is removed from the heat. Allow ten minutes for hard-boiled eggs. If you are going to eat the hard-boiled eggs later, cold, leave them on the stove (just below a simmer) for fifteen minutes.

Omelets

Omelets are fun to make and a great way to start the day. Use two eggs per person.

Beat all the eggs together in a bowl until the yolks and whites are thoroughly blended. Stir in about a tablespoon of water for every two eggs. You may use milk, but the omelet will not be as fluffy.

Now comes the challenge to your creativity! You may add nothing—or a great deal. To keep your omelet moist, add a tablespoon of finely chopped onion for every four eggs. Other ingredients that go well include small pieces of pre-fried bacon, finely chopped ham, or even chopped luncheon meat. Try small pieces of mushrooms or chopped or shredded cheese of your choosing. A tablespoon of mushrooms and/or a tablespoon of grated cheese for every two eggs are a good rule of thumb. Individual tastes differ, so experiment.

Use a non-stick frying pan or if you use a different skillet, coat it well with oil, butter, or margarine. Use medium-high heat. The size of the pan is important, because the egg mixture should be about one-third of an inch deep. Cover the pan for more uniform cooking. When the omelet is well browned on the bottom (about four minutes), flip it over. If you are using a large skillet with six or more eggs, it will be difficult to turn the omelet over unless you cut it into serving sizes in pie shapes and then you can turn one portion at a time. It may seem a little messy, but it will work.

Salt and pepper before serving, but let individuals add more if they wish. Have Tabasco or other hot sauces on the table for those who enjoy spicy foods.

Individual Omelets

These will take a little longer. Use a smaller pan, just large enough for two or three eggs. (Omelet pans are available.) When making individual omelets, you may want to fold the omelet over when it is brown on the bottom and place the added ingredients in the fold—like mushrooms, cheese, onions, jelly, etc.

Ingredients for "My Favorite Omelet"

Ingredients to serve one—to serve two, use 4 or 5 eggs:

    3 eggs
    ½ T chopped onion (heaping)
    2 slices of bacon—cut into ½ inch strips and pre-fried
    1 T shredded cheddar cheese
    1 T chopped mushrooms
    1 T water

Scrambled Eggs

Place the eggs in a bowl along with a teaspoon of water for every two eggs. Stir them with a fork or whisk until the whites and yolks are thoroughly blended. Pour the mixture into a pre-heated, non-stick skillet with a little oil or butter. If some other kind of pan is used, more lubricant is required.

Stir occasionally with your spatula until done. Again, cook them long enough so they are not "watery," but not so long that they get "rubbery." Season lightly and serve.

To make your eggs go farther, stir in chunks of bread (about ½-inch square) before you fry the eggs.

An entirely different taste is achieved by breaking the eggs directly into the pan and stirring gently as they fry.

Any of the omelet recipes may also be scrambled; just stir occasionally with the spatula to keep the eggs in small pieces.

Poached Eggs

Break the eggs onto a saucer and slide them carefully (so as not to break the yolks) into boiling water. Remove after three minutes with a large slotted spoon and serve on buttered toast. Let each season his own.

Minnesota Skillet Breakfast

Ingredients to serve one—double the amounts to serve two:

    1 red potato cut into bite-size chunks
    2 eggs, beaten
    ½ cup pork sausage (bulk type)
    1 small onion, chopped
    2 T cheddar cheese, grated or shredded
    3 T vegetable oil
    Dash each of salt and pepper

Combine all ingredients and fry in vegetable oil, stirring frequently.

Chicken Broth with Eggs

A little different way to enjoy eggs. Ingredients to serve one—double the amounts to serve two:

- 1 cup water
- 1 chicken bouillon cube
- 2 eggs
- 2 T chopped parsley
- 2 T grated cheese of your choosing
- Dash each of salt and pepper

Dissolve the bouillon cube in the water. Heat until bubbly—not boiling.

Beat together all other ingredients (until frothy).

Slowly pour the egg mixture into the broth, stirring as it is added. Let cook a minute or two without stirring—until the eggs are set.

Serve with croutons or toast.

Bacon

Bacon is best broiled, but watch it carefully so it doesn't burn. Turn when one side is done.

When frying bacon in a pan, use medium heat and fry both sides.

When preparing large quantities of bacon, just lay the pieces loosely in the pan. Stir the pieces around occasionally so they don't burn and they will "French fry" in their own grease. (I learned this technique from Alaskan guide Paul Carlson.)

Sausage Patties

Fry as you would hamburgers, but keep them small and fairly thin to ensure they are cooked all the way through. Use medium heat, turning once. To be sure they are cooked through, add a few drops of water at the end and cover the skillet; the steam will do the trick.

Pork Links

Fry over moderate heat with a little water in the pan. Cover the pan to finish them off; add a little water and the steam will make sure they are well cooked.

Breakfast Ham

Use pre-cooked ham. Slice it a little thinner than dinner ham. Don't over-cook; all you are really doing is warming it up.

Baking Powder Biscuits

Ingredients for 4 biscuits: If you are alone, eat two later:

> 1 cup flour
> 1 T (level) baking powder
> 1 t salt (level)
> 1 t sugar (level)
> ¼ stick of butter or margarine
> ½ cup milk

Sift together the dry ingredients (flour, baking powder, salt, and sugar). If you don't have a "sifter," shake them together (thoroughly) in a paper bag. Using your fingers, rub soft butter or margarine into the powdered ingredients until they are uniformly coated or sticky. Add the milk and work into a soft dough. Place the dough on waxed paper or a flour-covered board. Pat it out until it is uniformly about ¾-inch thick. Cut into squares (about two inches) or cut into circles—a cookie cutter or small cover will do. Reform the scraps and make these also into biscuits.

Arrange on a greased cookie sheet or heavy foil and place them in a preheated, very hot oven (450 degrees) for about 12 minutes or until brown. (Use a middle shelf in the oven.)

Blueberry Muffins

Enough to enjoy with breakfast for a week!

    1 egg
    ½ T butter (melted)
    2 cups flour
    3½ T baking powder
    1 cup milk
    ½ T salt
    2 T sugar
    1 cup blueberries

Add the baking powder and salt to the two cups of sifted flour (sift before measuring). Now place the milk in a bowl and add the sugar. Beat the egg into the milk; melt the butter and add it to the milk-egg mixture. Sift the dry ingredients into the liquid mixture. Add the blueberries and stir gently until the ingredients are uniformly dampened. Don't worry about the lumps in the mixture.

Pour the ingredients into a muffin pan and bake in a moderate oven for about twenty-five minutes or until a toothpick thrusts easily into the muffin and they are well browned.

Gourmet Oatmeal*

Ingredients for one-quart mix:

   1/3 cup dark brown sugar
   ½ T ground cinnamon
   1/16 T ground nutmeg
   3 cups old-fashioned oatmeal
   ½ cup finely diced pitted dates
   ½ cup finely diced dried apple
   1/3 cup raisins or craisins

Mix all ingredients in a large bowl. Stir well. Store in a quart jar and use as desired. Usually, one quart will make five nice servings. The mix keeps well and looks very nice on the countertop.

* *Courtesy Jerry Hayenga, Waite Park, MN*

Cocoa Mix*

20 qt. box dry milk (27 cups)
2 lbs. Nestles Quik
2 lbs. powdered sugar
20 oz. dry Coffee-mate

Mix together.

Use 1/3 cup of mix to one cup of water (or to taste).

Courtesy Jerry Hayenga, Waite Park, MN

CHAPTER 2
Starters

Apple Slices with Cheese

Ingredients to serve one—double the amounts to serve two:

1 large, hard, red apple (such as Winesap or Prairie Spy) cored and sliced
4 T mild cream cheese
2 T sour cream
1 T rum or brandy of your choice (optional)
1 t mustard

Core and slice each apple. Dip each slice in a glass of water in which a few drops of lemon juice have been dissolved (to prevent discoloring). Combine all other ingredients. Spread on apple slices.

Woodticks on a Popple Tree

Ingredients to serve one—double the amounts to serve two:

4 ribs of celery cut into 2-inch chunks
½ package cream cheese
½ cup raisins

Cut and clean the ribs from a stalk of celery. Then cut them into chunks about two inches long. Fill the indented sides of the celery pieces with cream cheese. Press 4 or 5 raisins into the cheese on each chunk.

Deep-fried, Battered Morel Mushrooms

Ingredients to serve one—double the amounts to serve two:

1 cup small morel mushrooms, dusted clean. If damp, pat dry with paper towel.
Prepare your favorite pancake or fish batter.

Immerse mushrooms in the batter and drop into hot oil (375 degrees).

Remove when a golden brown.

Stuffed Celery Pieces

Ingredients to serve one—double the amounts to serve two:

- 2 ribs celery. Cut into 3 or 4 inch chunks
- 3 oz. cream cheese
- 2 T chopped fresh mushrooms
- 2 slices thin bacon, broiled and crumbled
- 2 T chopped onion
- 3 T butter

Cut celery ribs into 3 or 4 inch chunks. Sauté the mushrooms in the butter. Blend together all ingredients and stuff celery.

Dates Stuffed with Cheese and Wrapped with Bacon

Ingredients to serve one—double the amounts to serve two:

12 pitted dates
½ package cream cheese
6 slices thin, lean bacon

Slice the dates open and stuff them with the cream cheese.

Meanwhile, broil the bacon strips until they are well done but not crisp. Cut each slice in half. Wrap each stuffed date with a piece of bacon and secure it with a toothpick.

Deep-fried Mushrooms with Melted Cheese Dip

Ingredients to serve one—double the amounts to serve two:

> 1 cup morel mushrooms, dusted clean.
> Thin pancake batter (about 1 1/2 cups)
> 1 T onion, chopped very fine
> 6 T sharp cheese of your choosing, melted

Prepare the pancake batter. Stir in chopped onion. Clean and dry mushrooms; leave whole or cut caps from stems. Dip mushrooms in batter and deep fat fry at 350 degrees. Dip mushrooms in melted cheese.

Eggs Stuffed with Smoked Fish

Ingredients to serve one—double the amounts to serve two:

3 hardboiled eggs
3 T smoked fish, chopped fine (salmon is my favorite)
2 T mayonnaise
1 T sour cream
Dash pepper

Thinly slice top off each egg so that they will stand on end. Cut eggs in half. Remove yolks and save. Combine smoked fish, mayonnaise, sour cream, yolks, and pepper in a blender.

Mound filling in each egg half.

Smoked Fish and Cucumber Spread

Ingredients to serve one—double the amounts to serve two:

1 cup flaked, smoked fish (salmon is my favorite)
½ cup cucumbers, chopped
½ cup mayonnaise
1 t (level) pepper (use white if available)

Mix thoroughly and refrigerate at least one hour.

Smoked Fish—Dill Spread

Ingredients to serve one—double the amounts to serve two:

1 cup flaked, smoked fish
4 T cream cheese
1 T lemon or lime juice
½ t pepper (white if available)
2 T mayonnaise
2 T dill weed

Mix ingredients thoroughly. Refrigerate. Serve on bread, toast, or crackers.

Guacamole Dip

Ingredients to serve one—double the amounts to serve two:

- 1 avocado, peeled, pitted, chopped, and mashed
- 4 T mayonnaise
- 1 T Worcestershire sauce
- 2 T chopped nuts of your choice

Blend all ingredients.

Shrimp Dip

Ingredients to serve one—double the amounts to serve two:

- 1 cup cooked, shelled shrimp, chopped
- 4 oz. cream cheese
- 1 t curry powder
- 1 t minced garlic
- 1 t minced onion

Combine all ingredients thoroughly. Refrigerate if not served immediately.

Cucumber Dip

Ingredients to serve one—double the amounts to serve two:

- 1 medium cucumber peeled, seeded, and diced fine
- 6 T plain yogurt
- 1 T lime or lemon juice
- 1 T fresh dill, chopped
- 1 T minced onion

Combine all ingredients thoroughly. Refrigerate before serving.

Hawaiian Spread

Ingredients to serve one—double the amounts to serve two:

- 1 cup crushed pineapple, drained, from the can
- 4 T cream cheese
- ½ cup Macadamia nuts, chopped

Mix thoroughly. For a more zesty flavor, add 3 chopped green onions.

Nutty Cheese Spread

Ingredients to serve one—double the amounts to serve two:

>   1 cup grated cheese (cheddar works well)
>   1/3 cup finely chopped nuts of your choosing
>   2 slices, bacon, fried crisp and chopped
>   4 T mayonnaise
>   2 T minced onion

Combine all ingredients thoroughly.

Marinated Olives

Ingredients to serve one—double the amounts to serve two:

>   ½ cup black, pitted olives, drained
>   1/3 cup olive oil
>   1 t rosemary
>   1 t thyme
>   1 t lemon juice

Drain olives. Stir together all ingredients. Let marinate, refrigerated, 48 hours.

Bruschetta Appetizer #1

Ingredients to serve one—double the amounts to serve two:

**1 slice (fairly thick) Italian or French bread (or whatever is handy)
1 medium tomato
1 clove garlic, minced
Six "rings" from a purple onion
1 T extra-virgin olive oil
Dash each of salt and pepper**

Chop tomato (not too fine). Mince the garlic. Brush bread with olive oil. Combine remaining ingredients. Spread over bread slice. Brown under the broiler in an oven. Watch carefully so it does not burn.

Bruschetta Appetizer #2

Ingredients to serve one—double the amounts to serve two:

   1 slice French or Italian bread (or whatever is handy)
   1 medium tomato, topped, seeded, and chopped fairly fine
   1 T extra-virgin olive oil
   1 toe garlic, minced
   Dash each of salt and pepper
   Cheese of your choosing, sliced thin and enough to cover bread

Place bread on a baking shake. Brush with oil. Combine remaining ingredients except cheese and spread to cover bread. Cover with one layer of cheese slices (mozzarella works well).

Bake in a preheated 350 degree oven until cheese melts or about 10 minutes.

Bruschetta Appetizer #3

Ingredients to serve one—double the amounts to serve two:

- 1 tomato, topped and chopped
- 2 green onions, chopped (or 2 T chopped onion)
- 12 black olives, pitted and sliced
- 1 t minced garlic
- 2 T grated cheese of your choosing
- 1 T olive oil

Spread oil on both sides of the bread and toast in a 350 degree oven. Make a paste by blending all other ingredients except the cheese. Spread paste on one side of the bread and sprinkle with cheese. Return to the oven briefly until the cheese melts.

Tomato Salsa

Ingredients to serve one—double the amounts to serve two:

- 1 large, ripe tomato, chopped
- 4 T chopped onion (preferably green)
- 2 T minced garlic
- 6 drops Tabasco sauce
- 1 t lemon or lime juice

Skin and chop the tomato. Chop the onion. Mince the garlic. Add the hot sauce a drop or two at a time. Combine the ingredients and let stand refrigerated at least one hour.

Garden Salsa

Ingredients to serve one—double the amounts to serve two:

- 1 vine-ripened tomato, chopped
- 4 green onions, chop both white and green parts
- 4 T chopped green pepper
- 1 T minced garlic

Combine all ingredients. Refrigerate.

Favorite Snack—Caramel Corn—Old Dutch Style*

Ingredients to serve a dozen or more:

1 package Old Dutch Puffcorn
1 cup butter
1 1/4 cup brown sugar
2/3 cup light corn syrup
1 t baking soda
1 cup nuts (whole cashews)

Preheat oven to 250 degrees.

Combine butter, brown sugar and corn syrup in a 2-quart saucepan. Cook on medium heat until mixture has melted. Add baking soda.

Pour popcorn and nuts into a large roasting pan. Pour caramel mixture over puffcorn and mix thoroughly. Place in oven for 45 minutes and stir every 10-12 minutes.

Remove from oven and place on waxed paper and break apart. Let cool.

*Courtesy Julia Hayenga, Cold Spring, MN

CHAPTER 3
Soups

Chilled Tomato Soup

Ingredients to serve one—double the amounts to serve two:

- 1 T extra-virgin olive oil
- 1 clove garlic, minced
- 2 T chopped onion
- 1 large tomato, topped and chopped
- 2 T chopped torn) basil leaves
- 1 T sugar
- 1 cup water
- 2 T seasoned croutons

Sauté the garlic and onion pieces in the oil for a few minutes (until the onion is clear).

Combine all ingredients. Use a food processor to make an almost smooth soup.

Chill in a refrigerator at least three hours.

Garnish with seasoned croutons.

Carrot Soup with Apple

Ingredients to serve one—double the amounts to serve two:

1 large carrot, sliced thin
½ apple, peeled, cored, and chopped
2 T chopped onion (preferably sweet)
1 t minced garlic
1½ cups water
1 chicken bouillon cube
¼ stick of butter, chipped
1 bay leaf
dash of pepper
2 T chopped parsley for garnish

Sauté the carrots, apple, onion, and garlic in the butter (or margarine). Transfer to a soup kettle. Add all other ingredients and bring to a boil. Reduce heat to simmer for 30 minutes or until carrot slices are tender. Remove bay leaf and purée. Return to kettle and heat until piping hot.

Fresh Green Pea Soup

Ingredients to serve one—double the amounts to serve two:

    2 slices bacon, fried crisp and broken into bits for garnish
    1/8 pound butter (1/2 stick) melted
    1 cup fresh (or frozen) green peas, shelled
    2 T onion, chopped fine
    dash each of salt and pepper
    1 cup chicken broth

Sauté onion and celery in melted butter until onion is translucent. Combine all ingredients in a soup pot (except bacon) and simmer about 10 minutes or until peas are tender. Force through a coarse sieve and cook until hot. Garnish with bacon bits.

Garlic and Onion Soup

Ingredients to serve one—double the amounts to serve two:

**1 medium onion peeled, and broken into rings
2 cloves garlic, minced
1 cup water
1 small can beef broth
½ cup white wine
dash each of salt and pepper
2 T grated cheese of your choosing for garnish**

Combine all ingredients except cheese in a soup pot and simmer 30 minutes. Serve piping hot. Garnish with grated cheese.

Duck Soup

Ingredients to serve one—double the amounts to serve two:

½ large duck (such as a mallard) or all of a small duck (such as a teal),
  de-boned and cut into bite-size pieces
1 medium potato, cut into bite-size chunks
1 carrot, chopped
1 rib celery, chopped
2 T raisins
1 T salt
Optional: ½ apple, cut bite-size

Place all ingredients in a soup pot and cover with water. Simmer for one hour or until meat is tender. Serve piping hot.

Baked Potato Soup

Ingredients to serve one—double the amounts to serve two:

    1 medium baked potato, let cool and cut and mash into small pieces
    2 T chopped onion
    2 T chopped celery
    2 t olive oil
    1 can cream of chicken soup, diluted with one can water
    dash each of salt and pepper
    2 pieces bacon, fried crisp in olive oil and broken into small pieces for garnish

Bake potato, let cool, cut and mash into small pieces.

Sauté chopped onion and celery in the olive oil.

Combine all ingredients except bacon bits in a soup pot. Simmer over medium heat until piping hot. Serve with bacon bits as garnish (could also use grated cheese of your choosing).

Beer Soup with Pasta or Egg Noodles

Ingredients to serve one—double the amounts to serve two:

- 1 cup cooked egg noodles or pasta of your choice
- 1/8 pound butter or margarine chips
- 1 t cinnamon
- dash each of salt and pepper
- 1 can warm beer of your choice
- Crouton-size pieces of bread (preferably rye)

As soon as the pasta or noodles have been drained, stir in the chips of butter or margarine until they melt. Stir in the spices. Pour in the beer. Heat until hot, but do not let boil. Garnish with bits of bread.

Creamy Cauliflower Soup

May substitue broccoli. Ingredients to serve one—double the amounts to serve two:

1 cup trimmed cauliflower, bite-size pieces
1½ cups water
1 chicken bouillon cube
3 T cream
Chopped parsley for garnish

Cover cauliflower pieces with water. Bring to a boil; remove from heat and let stand 2 minutes. Drain and rinse with cold water. Return cauliflower to kettle; add 1½ cups water and all ingredients except parsley. Bring to a boil, then reduce heat to simmer for 15 minutes. Let stand until cool enough to handle. Return to kettle and re-heat, but do not let boil. Garnish with parsley.

Zucchini Soup

Ingredients to serve one—double the amounts to serve two:

- 1 cup peeled and chopped zucchini squash
- 2 cloves garlic, minced
- 2 T chopped onion
- 2 T extra-virgin olive oil
- 1½ cups water
- 2 T torn basil leaves
- dash each of salt and pepper
- (Save some of the zucchini peel and cut into strips.)

Sauté garlic and onion in oil until onion is clear.

Add the water, salt and pepper and zucchini and bring to a boil, then reduce heat to simmer and cook until squash pieces are soft. (Stir every few minutes.)

Let cool, then add the basil and purée the soup in a blender.

Re-heat until piping hot. Serve with a couple of strips of squash peel floating on top.

CHAPTER 4
Salads

Smoked Fish Salad

Ingredients to serve one—double the amounts to serve two:

    1 cup smoked fish (salmon is my favorite)
    1 cup cooked potatoes, diced
    2 T minced green onions (both white and green parts)
    2 T olives (either black or green) pitted and sliced

    Ingredients for salad oil:
    2 T olive oil
    2 T white vinegar
    1 t mustard

Combine salad ingredients and chill for at least one hour. Meanwhile, prepare salad oil. Stir in salad oil when you are ready to enjoy salad. You may want to add a dash of salt and/or pepper.

Apple Salad with Bacon

Ingredients to serve one—double the amounts to serve two:

1 heaping cup torn lettuce
1 apple, sliced into narrow wedges
3 slices crisp, broiled bacon, broken into bits
2 T grated cheese of your choosing
2 T slivered almonds (optional)

Dressing ingredients:
Dressing of your choosing or:
1/3 cup sour cream
1/3 cup light mayonnaise
2 T catsup

Beet Salad

Ingredients to serve one—double the amounts to serve two:

- 1 medium-size pickled beet, chopped
- 1 small apple, peeled, cored, and chopped
- 1 small potato, peeled, cooked, and chopped
- 1 T chopped onion
- ½ cup sour cream
- 1 t prepared mustard

Combine all of the above, chill and serve.

Ham and Cheese Salad

Ingredients to serve one—double the amounts to serve two:

Bed of lettuce leaves
¼ pound thinly sliced, chopped ham
3 T ricotta cheese, crumbled
3 T chopped pecans
2 green onions, chopped (both green and white parts)

Ingredients for salad oil:
3 T honey
2 T wine (preferably red)
1 T mustard
2 T water
3 T canola oil

Combine salad ingredients and place on top of lettuce leaves. Combine salad oil ingredients and drizzle over salad.

Beet and Onion Salad

Ingredients to serve one—double the amounts to serve two:

- 1 medium beet, skin removed, sliced and baked (pickled beets are an option)
- 2 medium sweet (purple) onions, broken into rings
- A bed of your favorite greens
- 3 T chopped nuts (pecans, almonds, or walnuts work well)
- 2 T olive oil
- 2 or 3 T sherry vinegar or your favorite dressing

Skin the beet, slice, and bake in oil for about one hour, let cool.

Skin and break the onion into rings.

Using your favorite greens as a bed, stack the sliced beets, onion rings, and chopped nuts on top. Drizzle dressing on salad and enjoy.

Italian Salad*

Ingredients to serve one—double the amounts to serve two:

1 ripe tomato, topped and sliced
¼-inch thick slices of mozzarella cheese
As many leaves of basil as slices of cheese
Extra-virgin olive oil for drizzling
Salt and pepper

Layer alternate slices of tomato and cheese, adding a basil leaf between each. Drizzle the salad with olive oil and season with salt and pepper.

Courtesy Judy Jenkins, Staples, MN

Tomato and Cheese Salad

Ingredients to serve one—double the amounts to serve two:

	2 T lemon juice
	2 T extra-virgin olive oil
	Salt and pepper
	1 large tomato, topped and cut into bite-size pieces
	3 slices mozzarella cheese cut into bite-size pieces
	3 basil leaves torn into small pieces

Prepare a dressing by whisking together the oil, lemon juice, and a dash each of salt and pepper.

Stir together pieces of tomato, cheese, and basil. Drizzle with the dressing.

Garden Vegetable Salad

Ingredients to serve one—double the amounts to serve two:

- 1 tomato, topped and chopped
- 1 medium carrot, sliced thin
- 1 rib celery, sliced thin
- 3 T grated cheese of your choice
- 2 T extra-virgin olive oil
- 3 T wine or wine vinegar of your choosing
- 2 T parsley flakes
- Salt and pepper

Shake together olive oil, wine, and a dash each of salt and pepper.

Combine vegetables and cheese on a plate and drizzle with dressing.

Garnish with parsley flakes.

Pasta Salad with Shrimp

Ingredients to serve one—double the amounts to serve two:

- ¼ package (4 ounces) pasta of your choosing
- 4 to 6 pre-cooked shrimp
- 2 green onions, chopped, both white and green parts
- 1 rib celery, sliced thin
- 1 carrot, sliced thin
- 1 t salt
- 4 T white or red tartar sauce

Prepare pasta according to directions on the package. Drain and rinse with cold water through a sieve.

Combine all ingredients, cover with plastic and refrigerate at least two hours.

Bell Pepper Salad

Ingredients to serve one—double the amounts to serve two:

1 large bell pepper, may be either green or red
4 T olives, either green or black, pitted and sliced
1 T extra-virgin olive oil
1 garlic clove, minced
Dash each of salt and pepper
1 T chopped (or torn) basil leaves

Bake the pepper in a 300 degree oven for 20 minutes or until it turns brown, turning occasionally.

Remove from oven. Let cool and cut into bite-size strips.

Combine all ingredients in a bowl and toss until well coated with the olive oil. May serve at room temperature or after being refrigerated.

Potato Salad #1

Ingredients to serve one—double the amounts to serve two:

>   2 medium size potatoes, peeled, and then sliced or diced
>   1 rib celery, chopped
>   3 T chopped onion
>   1 strip bacon, fried crisp then broken into bits
>   2 T vinegar
>   Dash each of salt and pepper

Using a saucepan, cover the slices or diced potatoes with water and cook until done.

Fry the slice of bacon until crisp, then break into bits.

Combine the vinegar, salt, and pepper with the bacon drippings.

Combine all ingredients and serve either hot or cold.

Potato Salad with a Touch of Wine

Ingredients to serve one—double the amounts to serve two:

> 6 small new potatoes, sliced or diced (may leave skins on)
> 1 medium onion, peeled and broken into rings
> 1 rib celery, chopped
> 1 strip bacon, fried and broken into pieces
> ½ cup of a favorite wine
> Dash each of salt and pepper

Using a saucepan, cover sliced or diced potatoes with water and cook 20 minutes or until done.

Fry bacon meanwhile and break into bits. Pour water off potatoes and combine all ingredients. Serve either hot or cold.

Cabbage Salad

Ingredients to serve one—double the amounts to serve two:

- **1 heaping cup chopped cabbage**
- **1 small onion, peeled and chopped**
- **1 heaping T your favorite salad herbs, chopped (like basil, chives, or dill)**
- **3 T wine or wine vinegar**
- **1 T sugar**

Combine all ingredients just before serving.

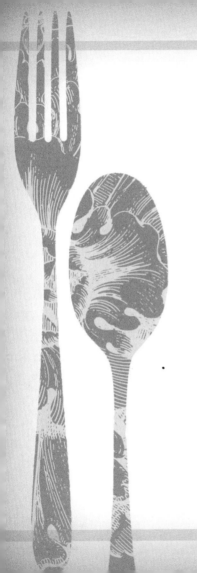

CHAPTER 5
Sandwiches

Sandwiches

You probably don't need a cookbook to tell you how to make sandwiches, but they are included here and briefly described to remind you of how many choices there are and to encourage you to make available different sandwiches each time you serve soup for lunch.

Hamburgers

An old reliable—especially with the kids. Hamburgers always "hit the spot" when served with potato chips and/or soup.

Hamburger patties, fried slowly on both sides, are best served on traditional hamburger buns. Season with salt and pepper. They can be "doctored up" by adding a little chopped onion or one-half envelope of dried onion soup mix to each pound of hamburger.

You may use the charcoal broiler—with barbecue sauce for seasoning—brushed on as the hamburgers broil.

Building a Burger

Start with a juicy, grilled beef patty and then add three or more (the only limitation is how wide you can open your mouth!) of the following ingredients:

Grilled bacon
Sliced onion
Sliced tomato
Catsup or mustard and/or garlic salt
Sliced cheese (cheddar works well)
Greens (lettuce is the old reliable)

The same ingredients will work for "sliders" (smaller buns).

Hot Dogs

Wieners can be broiled, boiled, or roasted over an open fire. They can be made extra-fancy by baking them in the oven (or over an open fire on a stick) with wrap-around strips of bread dough (from your grocer's dairy case).

Doctoring Those Hot Dogs

Option #1: Cut a deep length-wise cut in the wiener and fill the cut with your favorite cheese, then bake and enjoy in a bun.

Option #2: Boil, bake, or grill the wieners, insert each wiener in a bun, then dress with sliced bananas, chopped pineapple, and your favorite dressing.

Option #3: Wrap the wieners with slices of bacon and then bake or grill. Enjoy in a bun, dressed with catsup or mustard.

Option #4: Boil, bake, or grill the wieners. Place each in a bun and add your favorite chopped onion (green onions from the garden work well, both green and white parts). Add mustard or catsup.

Option #5: Last, but not least, add freshly cooked chili to the buns.

Brats

A favorite on the grill for most folks. Some want them heated through, but do not want the skin to break. Others like the skin to crack, making them dryer, but more spicy.

Some like sauerkraut stuffed in the bun along with the brat. Mustard, catsup, and hot spices should also be available.

Fish Sandwich

You can re-heat leftover fillets for this one or fry them fresh. Just cut the fillets "sandwich size," dip them in an egg wash (one egg stirred into a cup of water), roll them in cracker crumbs (or your favorite coating), season with lemon pepper and fry in oil a few minutes on each side. Spread the bread or buns with tartar sauce.

Mashed Potatoes on Brats

Ingredients to serve one—double the amounts to serve two:

2 brats, sliced length-wise (wieners may be substituted)
1 potato, peeled and chunked
2 T grated or shredded cheese (cheddar works well)
2 T milk
1 T butter or margarine, melted
Salt and pepper to taste

Boil the chunked potatoes in water in a covered saucepan for about 15 minutes of until done (check with a fork). Drain and return to the stove for a couple of minutes to dry the potatoes.

Slice the brats or wieners length-wise, but leave the halves attached with a little skin.

Mash the potatoes, milk, and butter together.

Spoon the mashed potatoes on top of the brats or wieners. Season lightly with salt and pepper. Sprinkle with the cheese.

Bake in a pre-heated 375 degree oven for about 10 minutes or until the cheese melts.

Smoked Meat Sandwich

Ingredients to serve one—double the amounts to serve two:

Use a variety of breads, apply the chosen meats, and serve them open-faced.

Here are some possibilities: (Try one slice per person)

Thin slices of dried beef
Thin slices of smoked fish
Top with one hardboiled egg, finely chopped and blended with 2 T mayonnaise.

Tomato—Cheese Sandwich

Ingredients to serve one—double the amounts to serve two:

- 2 slices of bread
- 2 slices mozzarella cheese (or cheese of your choosing)
- 1 tomato, large enough for thick slices to cover bread
- 2 T extra-virgin olive oil
- Dash each of salt and pepper

Combine all ingredients except olive oil. Make into a sandwich. Brush both sides of bread with oil.

Place in oven under the broiler. Brown both side. Make sure cheese has melted.

Open-face Egg Sandwich

Ingredients to serve one—double the amounts to serve two:

**1 slice bread of your choosing (the thicker the better)
1 or 2 eggs (whatever it takes to cover the bread) crushed
1 small tomato—topped, chopped, and crushed
4 T extra-virgin olive oil
Salt and pepper
Garlic salt
2 T grated cheese of your choosing**

Place 2 T oil in a skillet and fry eggs (on one side only if you like the yolk runny).

Sprinkle eggs with salt, pepper, and garlic salt.

Toast bread. Brush the top side of the toast with the remaining olive oil.

Sprinkle with crushed tomatoes. Top with the fried egg(s).

Herring and Potato Sandwich

A Scandinavian treat. Ingredients to serve one—double the amounts to serve two:

1 cup pickled herring, chopped very fine
1 medium potato, boiled and chopped fine
2 slices rye bread, spread with mayonnaise
Lettuce, enough to cover a slice of bread

Ham Sandwich

Using pre-cooked ham

Ham is traditionally served on rye or wheat bread, which may be toasted. Mustard goes well with ham, but mayonnaise is also good. If the ham is heated it will have more flavor.

Flaked Fish Sandwich

You may use leftover fish or fresh, but be sure it is cooked. Flake the cooked fish with a fork or chop it. For one cup of flaked fish, stir in 3 T sweet pickle relish, 3 T of mayonnaise, and 2 T minced onion. Spread generously between slices of bread or buns, (toasted).

BLTs (Bacon, Lettuce, and Tomato)

Here's an old standby that will make a good lunch all by itself. Traditionally, the bread should be toasted. Sandwiched between the slices should be a couple of lettuce leaves, thick slices of tomatoes, and several strips of broiled bacon. Use butter, margarine, or mayonnaise on the slices of toast.

Grilled Spicy Chicken on a Bun

Ingredients to serve one—double the amounts to serve two:

1 chicken breast half, skinned and boneless
1 hamburger bun, toasted lightly
1 slice cheddar or other sharp cheese
1 t crushed peppercorns
Dash salt
Dash chili powder (optional)
Vegetable oil
Mayonnaise

Flatten the breast for more even thickness. Brush both sides of the fillet with oil. Press the crushed peppercorns into one side. Sprinkle both sides of the fillet with the seasoned salt and chili powder. Grill each side about 5 minutes. Toast the inside surface of the bun halves on the grill for a couple of minutes or until light brown. Spread bun surfaces with mayonnaise (or butter) and serve with a slice of cheese on top of each piece of chicken.

Toasted Club Sandwich

Ingredients to serve one—double the amounts to serve two:

3 slices bread, toasted
1 slice cooked ham, about 1/3 inch thick
1 slice Swiss cheese
enough pre-cooked turkey or chicken pieces to cover a slice of bread
2 pieces broiled bacon
1 slice sweet onion
mayonnaise, mustard, creamed horseradish

Spread 1 slice of toast with mustard, 1 with mayonnaise, and 1 with creamed horseradish. Layer all other ingredients between the three slices of toast. Cut each sandwich in half diagonally.

Lunchmeat Sandwiches

Your family or guests will enjoy making their own. Make at least two kinds of bread available, a variety of luncheon meats, pickles, sliced tomatoes, lettuce, sliced onions, and a variety of spreads.

Apple Club Sandwich*

Ingredients to serve one—double the amounts to serve two:

- 2 slices rye bread
- 2 thin slices turkey or chicken
- 2 thin slices ham
- 4 thin slices peeled and cored apple
- 2 T mayonnaise
- 2 lettuce leaves
- 2 T mustard

Spread mustard and mayonnaise on rye bread. Stack remaining ingredients between slices of bread.

*Courtesy Beth Chandler, Waite Park, MN

CHAPTER 6
Side Dishes

Zucchini with Wine

Ingredients to serve one—double the amounts to serve two:

- 1 medium zucchini squash, cut into half-inch sections
- 2 T extra-virgin olive oil
- 4 T red wine
- 2 T chopped parsley

Sauté the zucchini in the oil. Brown the sections on both sides. Add wine and cook until wine evaporates, turning each section at least once.

Sprinkle with parsley flakes as a garnish.

More Zucchini

Ingredients to serve one—double the amounts to serve two:

- 1 medium zucchini, sliced cross-wise (should equal one cup)
- 1 clove garlic, minced
- 2 T chopped onion
- 3 T extra-virgin olive oil
- 1 small tomato, topped, seeded, and diced
- 2 leaves basil, torn into small pieces
- 3 T shredded cheese of your choosing
- Dash each of salt and pepper

Sauté the squash in the oil until soft. Add garlic and onion and continue a couple more minutes.

Add all other ingredients and continue cooking and stirring until cheese melts.

Dandelion Greens

Ingredients to serve one—double the amounts to serve two:

1 quart greens, cut into two or three inch pieces, discard lower stems
1 clove garlic, minced
4 or 5 red pepper flakes
3 T olive oil
Dash of salt

Put greens in a pot. Cover with water. Add a dash or two of salt. Cook 8 or 10 minutes or until greens are tender. Rinse with cold water.

Add olive oil to a skillet. Sauté the minded garlic and pepper flakes until a light brown. Add greens and sprinkle with another dash of salt. Continue cooking for another 5 minutes, stirring every once in awhile, until greens are well covered with oil.

Fried Green Tomatoes

Ingredients to serve one—double the amounts to serve two:

> 2 medium green tomatoes, sliced thin (no more than half an inch)
> 1 egg
> ½ cup water
> 4 T cornmeal
> 4 T flour
> 4 T grated cheese
> 4 T olive oil
> 1 leaf basil, chopped or torn fine
> ½ t garlic salt

Whisk together the egg and water. Combine all other items except the olive oil in another bowl. Dip each slice first in the egg-water mixture and then in the dry ingredients. Fry the tomato slices in the olive oil—4 or 5 minutes on each side until a golden brown. Let dry on a paper towel; serve warm.

Summer Vegetable Side Dish

Ingredients to serve one—double the amounts to serve two:

- Eggplant, two ½ inch slices
- Zucchini, two ½ inch cross-cut slices
- 3 cherry-size tomatoes, halved, or one medium tomato, quartered
- 1 clove garlic, minced
- 6 rings purple sweet onion
- ¼ sweet green pepper, seeded and cut into bite-size strips
- 3 T extra-virgin olive oil
- 4 t red wine
- 1 T flour combined with a dash each of salt and pepper

Dust the eggplant and zucchini with the flour mixture and sauté in the oil, both sides (about 5 or 6 minutes per side). Add the garlic the last minute.

Place the squash strips on a plate and sprinkle with remaining ingredients.

Squash Side Dish

Ingredients to serve one—double the amounts to serve two:

- 1 heaping cup of peeled and sliced squash of your choosing
- 1 clove garlic, minced
- 2 T extra-virgin olive oil
- 2 basil leaves, torn into small pieces
- 4 T grated cheese of your choice (mozzarella works well)

In a heavy, nonstick skillet, sauté and squash pieces in the olive oil over medium heat for about 5 minutes or until squash is soft, stirring all the time. Add the garlic and stir a couple more minutes.

Remove from heat and stir in basil and cheese. Serve with butter or butter substitute.

Red Cabbage Side Dish

Ingredients to serve one—double the amounts to serve two:

1 cup shredded red cabbage
½ cup water
½ cup chopped apple
2 t sugar
Dash each of salt and allspice

Mashed Potatoes with Blue Cheese

Ingredients to serve one—double the amounts to serve two:

- 1 potato, peeled and diced
- 4 T blue cheese, crumbled (other kinds of cheese may be substituted)
- 3 T milk
- 4 T chopped onion
- 4 T melted butter

Boil the diced potatoes about 20 minutes, drain off water and return potatoes to the pan and stir to dry. Mash together all ingredients. Serve hot.

Mashed Potatoes and Browned Onions

Ingredients to serve one—double the amounts to serve two:

    1 potato, peeled and diced
    1 small onion, peeled and broken into rings
    ½ cup cream (preferably sour)
    4 T melted butter
    Dash each of salt and pepper

Boil diced potatoes in a saucepan for about 20 minutes or until done. Discard water and return potato chunks to dry pan for a few minutes until dry. Sauté the onion rings in the butter until brown. Combine all ingredients and serve hot.

German Hot Cabbage

Ingredients to serve one—double the amounts to serve two:

   1 cup shredded cabbage
   ½ cup grated, peeled, raw potato
   2 pieces bacon, fried crisp and broken into small pieces

Cook cabbage and potato in 2 cups salted water for 15 minutes; drain.

Combine drained cabbage and potato and stir in bacon bits.

Serve hot.

Fried Potatoes

Ingredients to serve one—double the amounts to serve two:

1 large potato, peeled and sliced (about 1/8 inch thick)
1 small onion, peeled and broken into rings
¼ cup olive oil
Dash each of salt and pepper and/or other spices, such as dry mustard or dill

Fry the sliced potatoes and onion rings in the olive oil, uncovered, for about 40 minutes or until done.

Fold in the spices. Serve hot.

Zesty Corn on the Cob

Flavoring ingredients for two cobs, husks removed:

- 2 T melted butter
- 2 T honey
- Dash each of salt and pepper
- ¼ t paprika
- 1 t hot pepper sauce

Combine all seasoning ingredients in a saucepan and heat until butter is melted. Brush cobs with the seasonings several times while roasting and turning on an open grill.

Fried Potatoes with Bacon Bits

Ingredients to serve one—double the amounts to serve two:

    1 potato, sliced, with skin off or on, pre-cooked
    1 slice bacon, fried crisp
    1 T chopped onion
    2 T vegetable oil

Fry the bacon in the oil until crisp. Break into bit. Add all other ingredients to the oil and cook a few minutes until contents are hot.

Rose Germann's Baseball Dumplings*

Ingredients to serve 6 (as a side dish):

6 large potatoes, peeled, quartered, cooked, and mashed
4 slices toast (bite-size pieces)
2 cups flour
Salt
¼ pound butter, melted

Boil potatoes, mash and let cool. Using hands, mix potatoes and toast. Mix flour with potatoes to form a ball about the size of a baseball.

You may need more flour. Put balls in boiling salted water for 15 to 20 minutes. When they float to the top, use a slotted spoon to take out.

Brown butter and pour over balls.

Sometimes Rose would use 1 or 2 eggs and 1 t baking powder.

*In memory of Rose Germann, Staples, MN

Sauce for Your Steak

Ingredients to serve one—double the amounts to serve two:

A steak of your choosing
2 T extra-virgin olive oil
1 garlic clove, minced
3 T chopped onion
4 chopped hot red pepper flakes (optional)
4 T pitted and chopped black olives
4 T pitted and chopped green olives (if stuffed, leave stuffing in)

Sauté all sauce ingredients in the olive oil until onion is translucent. Pour hot sauce over cooked steaks.

CHAPTER 7
Main Dishes

Baked Freshwater Fish Fillets with Tomato Sauce

Ingredients to serve one—double the amounts to serve two:

- ½ pound fillets (bass works well)
- 1 #2 can crushed tomatoes (preferably Italian-style)
- 3 T torn basil leaves
- 1 T capers
- 2 T lemon juice
- 1 dash each of salt and pepper

Line a baking dish with foil. Make a sauce of all the ingredients except the fish. Pour half the sauce into the pan. Place the fillets in the sauce. Cover the fillets with the rest of the sauce. Bake in a preheated 350 degree oven until the fillets flake easily with a fork. (Use the same amount of sauce for one pound of fillets for two.)

Pasta with Shrimp

Ingredients to serve one—double the amounts to serve two:

- 4 oz. (1/4 package) pasta of your choosing (linguini works well)
- 6 large shrimp (more if they are smaller)
- 1 small can mushrooms (drained, 4 oz.)
- 4 green onions, chopped, both white and green parts
- ½ stick butter, melted (1/8 pound)
- 4 T olive oil
- 1 cup white wine or cream

Prepare pasta according to directions on the package. Sauté the shrimp, onions, and mushrooms in the butter and olive oil. Stir in the wine or cream the last couple of minutes so that the sauce will be hot when it is poured over the cooked pasta.

Mashed Potatoes with Cream Cheese and Herbs

Ingredients to serve one—double the amounts to serve two:

- 1 large potato, peeled and quartered
- 4 T cream cheese, softened
- 4 T butter or substitute, softened
- Dash each of salt and pepper
- 2 basil leaves, torn into small pieces
- 2 T chopped parsley for garnish
- 4 T milk or cream

Boil the quarters of the potato in a saucepan for 15 minutes or until done.

Drain potatoes and place in a bowl. Mash until smooth. Add all ingredients except parsley and beat until well blended. Top with parsley for garnish.

Spicy Spuds

Ingredients to serve one—double the amounts to serve two:

    2 medium red potatoes, skins on, cut into bite-size chunks
    4 T extra-virgin olive oil
    1 clove garlic, minced
    4 T minced onion
    1 t red pepper flakes
    1 t salt

Combine the last 4 ingredients in a bowl. Brush the potato chunks with the olive oil. Toss a few chunks of potato at a time into the bowl and coat with the spice mixture. Arrange potato chunks on a greased cookie sheet, sides not touching.

Bake in a preheated 350 oven for 45 minutes or until easily penetrated with a fork.

Drizzle any leftover olive oil on the potato chunks before serving.

Seasoned Potatoes

Ingredients to serve one—double the amounts to serve two:

   1 large potato, cut in two lengthwise
   2 T olive oil
   1 t Italian seasoning
   Dash each of salt and pepper
   1 t paprika

Make several half-inch cuts into the cut surfaces of the potato. Brush some of the oil on the cuts.

Brush some of the oil on a cookie or baking sheet. Place the potato halves on the cookie sheet, cuts down. Bake 45 minutes at 350 degrees.

Mix the remainder of the oil with the seasonings. Turn the potatoes over with a spatula and brush with the seasoned oil. Bake another 45 minutes until done.

Potato with Herbs on the Grill

You can also cook this in an oven. Ingredients to serve one—double the amounts to serve two:

- 1 large potato, quartered, if skin is edible, leave it on
- 1 clove garlic, minced
- 2 basil leaves, torn into small pieces
- 1 thyme, chopped fine
- 2 T chopped parsley
- Salt and pepper, a couple of dashes of each
- 2 T extra-virgin olive oil

Combine the seasonings in a bowl. Brush the potato sections with the olive oil and roll sections in the bowl of seasonings.

Place the potato sections between two pieces of heavy foil. Place on top of a medium-hot grill or in a 325 degree oven. Cook for 20 minutes, then turn over and cook for another 10 minutes or until potato may be easily penetrated with a fork.

Serve with leftover oil.

Cheese-coated Panfish

Ingredients to serve one—double the amounts to serve two:

    ½ pound panfish fillets
    4 T all-purpose flour
    1 beaten egg
    4 T dry bread crumbs
    Dash each of salt and pepper
    4 T grated cheese of your choosing
    4 T cooking oil of your choice

Combine beaten egg, salt, pepper, bread crumbs, and cheese. Coat each fillet with this mixture. Fry fillets on each side in oil in a hot skillet.

Fillets in Beer Batter

Fillets should be about one-half inch thick. Remove skin and bones.

Pour ½ cup of beer into a bowl and let stand until flat.

Or add ½ cup of 7-up to the beer just before frying.

Or refrigerate the beer while it stands overnight.

Next day, combine the beer with:

> 1 cup of flour and/or bread crumbs
>
> 1 egg, beaten
>
> Dash each of salt and pepper

Dip fillets into above mixture and then fry on both sides in cooking oil in a hot skillet until brown.

Doctoring Your Favorite Beer Batter Recipe*

Use your favorite beer batter recipe, but use fresh cold beer.

Add 1 T baking soda
Add Old Bay seasoning to taste.

Courtesy Greg Hayenga, Cold Spring, MN

Baked Panfish with Parsley and Dill

Ingredients to serve one—double the amounts to serve two:

½ pound panfish fillets (heads, entrails, scales, and skin removed)
Cover bottom of a baking dish with ¼ cup chopped parsley and arrange fillets on top
Top fillets with 2 T chopped parsley and 2 T chopped dill
Pour ½ inch hot water around fillets

Bake at 350 degrees for 20-25 minutes.

Sauerbraten

Ingredients to serve one—double the amounts to serve two:

> 1 small beef roast, about a pound (a cooked roast keeps well, consider two pounds and save half to eat later, in which case, double the following amounts)
> Enough butter or oil to brown the roast
> Marinade ingredients: 1 cup red wine or red wine vinegar, 1 onion, chopped, 1 rib celery, chopped, 1 bay leaf

Combine marinade ingredients in a saucepan, bring to a boil, let simmer 5 minutes. Place roast in a covered glass container; pour the marinade over it. Let roast sit in refrigerator two days, turning 2 or 3 times a day.

Remove roast; pat dry and brown in oil or butter. Save marinade. Place roast in a Dutch oven; pour marinade over it. Cover and cook over low heat until tender.

Cube Steak with Caramelized Onions

Ingredients to serve one—double the amounts to serve two:

>1 cheaper cut of beef steak, between ¾ pound and a pound (tenderized)
>1 medium yellow onion, peeled and chopped (not too fine)
>1/8 pound of butter (1/2 stick)
>Salt and pepper to taste
>Canola oil
>Chopped chives for garnish

Tenderize the steak with a mallet designed for that purpose or use the butt end of a knife.

Melt the butter in a heavy frying pan (cast iron works well) and sauté the chopped onion over medium heat. Season with salt and pepper. Remove onions and add a thin layer of vegetable oil. Fry the steak over high heat, about 6 minutes on each side. Serve the steaks covered with onions and chives.

Potato Pancakes with Apple

A slightly different recipe. Ingredients to serve one—double the amounts to serve two:

> 1 cup grated or finely chopped potatoes
> 4 T grated or finely chopped apple
> 1 T flour
> 1 egg
> Dash each of salt and pepper
> Oil for frying

Combine all ingredients. Preheat about ¼ inch oil in a skillet. Spoon the batter into the skillet, making three pancakes. Using a spatula, after about three minutes, flip the cakes over.

"Doctored" Sauerkraut #1

Ingredients to serve one—double the amounts to serve two:

**1 cup canned or cooked sauerkraut
½ cup white wine
4 T brown sugar**

Combine ingredients and let simmer about 30 minutes.

"Doctored" Sauerkraut #2

Ingredients to serve one—double the amounts to serve two:

   1 cup canned or cooked sauerkraut
   4 T brown sugar
   2 T chopped onion
   1 small apple, cored and chopped
   4 cloves
   1 T cooking oil

Sauté onion in cooking oil. Add all remaining ingredients to the pan and continue to heat about 30 minutes. Serve hot or cold.

Sauerkraut and Wiener Casserole

Ingredients to serve one—double the amounts to serve two:

1 cup of sauerkraut
2 wieners, cut into bite-size chunks
½ cup water
2 T brown sugar
1 small potato, peeled and grated

Combine sauerkraut, wiener chunks, water, and brown sugar. Simmer 30 minutes. Add the grated potatoes and cook another 30 minutes.

Beef Stroganoff (German-style)

Ingredients to serve one—double the amounts to serve two:

- 1 cup tender steak, cut bite-size
- 1 cup broth or consommé
- 3 T sliced mushrooms (your choice)
- 3 T sour cream (if available)
- 4 T broken onion rings
- 3 T all-purpose flour
- 3 T butter

Roll the steak pieces in the flour and brown in the butter. Add all other ingredients except sour cream and simmer 20 minutes or until meat is tender. Add sour cream. Add a dash each or salt and pepper.

Serve over rice, potatoes, or pasta.

Potato Pancakes

Ingredients to serve one—double the amounts to serve two:

1 heaping cup mashed potatoes
½ stick butter or margarine, melted
3 T green onions, chopped, both white and green parts
1 clove garlic, minced
1 egg
4 T olive oil

Sauté the minced garlic in the butter a couple of minutes. Combine all ingredients with the melted butter and garlic. Spoon the mixture onto a preheated skillet or griddle that has been greased with the oil, forming three small or two large pancakes. Fry until brown on both sides.

Potato Dumplings

Ingredients to make four dumplings—double the amounts to make eight:

    1 cup raw potatoes, peeled and grated
    1 cup mashed potatoes (leftovers work well)
    1 heaping T flour
    1 egg
    1 t cornstarch
    1 t salt

Test by making one dumpling first.

Combine all ingredients. Meanwhile place a soup pot of water on the stove and bring it to boiling.

Make one dumpling—about the size of a half dollar. Drop it into the boiling water. If the dough starts to disintegrate, it means it is too soft. Add another teaspoon of cornstarch. When you have added enough cornstarch so the dough holds together, dump all the half-dollar size dumplings into the boiling water.

After about 5 minutes, test for doneness. Serve with bacon or butter or gravy.

Pork Chop with Wine Sauce

Ingredients to serve one—double the amounts to serve two:

- 1 pork chop (with or without bone)
- 1 clove minced garlic
- 2 T minced onion
- 2 T extra-virgin olive oil
- 2 T melted butter
- 1 small sweet green or red pepper, seeded and cut into strips
- ½ cup white wine

Rub both sides of the chop with the minced garlic and onion. Sauté the chop on both sides in the oil. Remove the chop and set aside covered with foil or a towel.

Add wine, butter, and pepper strips to the skillet. Bring to a oil, stirring all the while. Place the chop on a plate and pour the sauce over it.

Pasta with Leftover Ham

Ingredients to serve one—double the amounts to serve two:

- ¼ of a 16-ounce package of pasta of your choosing
- 1 cup bite-size chunks of ham
- 1 cup fresh peas
- 2 T shredded cheese of your choosing
- 4 T cream
- 3 T extra-virgin olive oil

Prepare the pasta according to the directions on the package. Meanwhile, sauté the ham and the peas.

When the pasta is done, combine with the other ingredients. Serve hot.

Spaghetti with Meat Sauce

Ingredients to serve one—double the amounts to serve two:

> 2/3 cup Italian sausage or hamburger or buy link sausage and remove casings
> ¼ package of spaghetti (4 oz.) or pasta of your choosing
> ½ cup crushed tomatoes (may use canned)
> 2 T diced onion
> 1 garlic clove, minced
> 4 basil leaves cut or torn into strips
> 2 T grated cheese of your choosing
> 2 T extra-virgin olive oil

Sauté the onion, garlic, and basil leaves in the oil. Crumble the sausage and add to the skillet, stirring until ingredients are browned. Add the tomatoes and continue to cook 10 minutes. Meanwhile, prepare the pasta according to directions on the package. Add the grated cheese and pour over cooked pasta.

Spaghetti with Anchovies

Ingredients to serve one—double the amounts to serve two:

- ¼ package of spaghetti (4 oz.)
- 1 cup diced or crushed tomatoes
- 2 T olive oil
- 1 garlic clove, minced
- 1 small (2 oz. can) anchovies, chopped
- 4 T sliced black or green olives (pitted)
- 1 t capers (optional)
- 1 T chopped parsley for garnish (optional)

Sauté the garlic in the olive oil. Add tomatoes and cook over medium heat 10 minutes. In the meantime, prepare the spaghetti of pasta of your choosing according to directions on the package. Add other ingredients (except parsley) to the sauce and continue to cook.

Drain pasta and mix well with the sauce. Garnish with chopped parsley.

Chicken and Pasta Casserole

Great for leftovers. Ingredients to serve one—double the amounts to serve two:

1 cup cooked chicken, chopped into small pieces
1 cup cooked pasta of your choosing
1 cup milk
1 small can sliced mushrooms
3 T grated cheese of your choosing

Combine all ingredients in an oven-safe casserole dish with grated cheese scattered on top. Bake in a preheated 350 degree oven for 15 minutes.

Chicken Thigh Pasta*

Great for leftover chicken. Ingredients to serve one—double the amounts to serve two:

> ¼ package pasta of your choosing (4 oz.)
> 1 cup cut-up chicken thighs (small pieces)

Brown chicken in olive oil and butter.

> Add 2 T chopped onion
> Add ½ t each of chopped basil, oregano, and garlic, and continue cooking until onion is translucent.
> Add 1 medium tomato, topped and chopped and continue cooking until piping hot.

In the meantime, prepare the pasta according to directions on the package.

Pour the chicken mixture over the pasta.

*Adapted from recipe by Tom Honek, Staples, MN. As found in Italian Home Cooking Cookbook.

Pasta with Mushroom Sauce

Ingredients to serve one—double the amounts to serve two:

    4 ounces (¼ pkg.) pasta of your choosing
    1 small can sliced mushrooms
    3 T olive oil
    1 T chopped thyme
    2 green onions, chopped, both white and green parts
    2 T grated cheese of your choosing
    Dash each of salt and pepper
    ½ cup cream

Prepare pasta according to directions on the package.

Sauté all other ingredients except cream in the olive oil.

Add cream and continue to cook until piping hot.

Spaghetti with Bacon and Eggs

Ingredients to serve one—double the amounts to serve two:

    ¼ pkg. (4 oz.) spaghetti or pasta of your choosing
    2 eggs
    2 slices bacon, cut bite-size
    3 T grated cheese of your choosing
    3 T olive oil
    Dash each of salt and pepper

Prepare pasta according to directions on the package.

Fry the bacon pieces in the olive oil. When crisp, remove from pan and set aside. Save olive oil and bacon fat.

Beat together eggs, salt, pepper, and grated cheese.

Combine all ingredients and stir into the cooked pasta until well coated. Serve hot.

Spaghetti Sauce with Bacon

Ingredients to serve one—double the amounts to serve two:

¼ package (4 oz.) spaghetti or pasta of your choosing
2 thick slices bacon, cut into bite-size pieces
2 T olive oil
2 T chopped onion
1 t minced garlic
1 #2 can crushed tomatoes (preferably Italian-style), may substitute fresh tomatoes
2 T grated cheese of your choosing
Optional – ¼ t red pepper flakes

Sauté the bacon pieces in the oil. Set aside bacon pieces; discard bacon grease.

Sauté the onion and garlic in the oil (until onion is translucent).

Add all ingredients to the skillet and cook over medium heat until piping hot.

Meanwhile, prepare the pasta according to directions on the package.

Pasta Sauce without Meat

Ingredients to serve one—double the amounts to serve two:

    ¼ package pasta of your choosing (4 oz.)
    1 #2 can crushed tomatoes (preferably Italian-style), may substitute fresh tomatoes
    2 T chopped onion
    1 T minced garlic
    2 T olive oil
    1-4-inch stalk celery, sliced very thin
    1 small carrot, sliced very thin
    1 basil leaf, torn into thin strips
    Dash each of salt and pepper

In a skillet, in oil, sauté onion, garlic, celery, and carrot until onion is translucent. Add basil, salt, and pepper, stirring well.

Add tomatoes and continue to stir and cook until sauce starts to thicken.

Meanwhile, prepare pasta according to directions on the package.

Tortellini with Nuts

Ingredients to serve one—double the amounts to serve two:

¼ package cheese tortellini (¼ pound) taken from your grocer's refrigerated display case
¼ cup chopped nuts of your choosing (walnuts or pecans work well)
¼ stick butter, sliced thin
1 T shredded Parmesan cheese (or cheese of your choosing)
Dash each of salt and pepper
2 T minced parsley

Prepare the tortellini according to directions on the package.

Meanwhile, melt the butter, then stir together all ingredients except the cheese. Combine all ingredients with the hot pasta and sprinkle the cheese on top.

Fettuccine Alfredo

Ingredients to serve one—double the amounts to serve two:

> ¼ package of fettuccine (4 oz.) or pasta of your choosing
> 1/8 pound (half stick) of butter, sliced into small pieces and softened
> 3 T grated cheese of your choosing
> 1 small can mushrooms, drained
> Dash each of salt and pepper

Prepare pasta according to directions on the package. Drain.

Add all other ingredients to the cooked pasta and toss until pasta pieces are well covered. Serve hot.

Leftover Chicken Cacciatore

Ingredients to serve one—double the amounts to serve two:

1 cup leftover, bite-size, cooked pieces of chicken
1 Italian link sausage, cut into bite-size pieces
2 T extra-virgin olive oil
1 tomato, topped and diced
1 garlic clove, minced
3 T Italian salad dressing
Dash each of salt and pepper

Sauté the Italian sausage pieces in the olive oil. After a few minutes, stir in all other ingredients and cook until piping hot.

Lunch from the Garden

Ingredients to serve one—double the amounts to serve two:

> ¼ package pasta of your choosing (¼ pound), cooked according to directions on the package
> 1 cup green peas (no pods)
> 2 garden green onions, chopped, both green and white parts
> 1 garlic clove, minced
> 2 T virgin olive oil
> Half a dozen hot red pepper flakes (optional)
> Dash each of salt and pepper
> 4 T grated cheese of your choosing
> ½ cup water

Prepare the pasta. Meanwhile, sauté the garlic in the olive oil. Add all other ingredients to make a sauce.

Cook until piping hot, stirring all the while.

Drain the pasta and place on a plate. Top with the sauce.

Pork Steak with Wine Sauce

Also works well with most any cuts of meat. Ingredients to serve one—double the amounts to serve two:

- ½ pound pork steak or chop with bone removed
- 2 T extra-virgin olive oil
- ½ cup canned or uncooked mushrooms
- 1 green onion, chopped, both green and white parts
- 6 stalks asparagus, trimmed and cut bite-size
- 2 basil leaves, cut into strips
- ½ cup white wine of your choosing
- Salt and pepper

Season both sides of the meat with salt and pepper. Sauté both sides of the meat in the olive oil over medium heat for about 4 minutes on each side. Remove meat and cover with foil or a towel.

Add all other ingredients (except the wine) to the skillet and cook until the asparagus is tender. (Use more oil if necessary.) Stir occasionally. Add the wine and continue cooking and stirring another two minutes. Serve hot wine sauce over the meat.

Sausage – Bean Dinner

Ingredients to serve one—double the amounts to serve two:

- ½ pound Italian pork sausages
- 1 large tomato, topped, seeded, and chopped
- 1 clove garlic, minced
- 3 T chopped sweet onion
- 2 T extra-virgin olive oil
- 1 bay leaf
- 2 T chopped parsley
- 2 basil leaves torn into narrow strips
- ½ can (14 oz.) white beans
- Dash each of salt and pepper

Sauté the garlic and the onion in oil in a large skillet. Add all other ingredients, including the liquid from the beans (but not the beans). Cook over medium heat, stirring occasionally, for 30 minutes. Add the beans and continue to cook for another 10 minutes. Discard the bay leaves.

Italian Sausage Chunks with Vegetables

Ingredients to serve one—double the amounts to serve two:

 1 medium potato, cut into bite-size chunks and boiled
 ½ medium sweet onion, broken into rings
 3 T chopped bell pepper, either green or red
 2/3 pound Italian sausages, cut into bite-size chunks
 3 T olive oil

Boil the potato chunks until done.

Meanwhile, sauté all other ingredients in the olive oil in a skillet until piping hot.

Stir in the hot potato chunks. Drain off oil and serve hot.

Fettuccine with Bacon Bits

Ingredients to serve one—double the amounts to serve two:

- ½ package fettuccine (4 ounces)
- 3 slices thick bacon, cut into bite-size pieces
- ½ cup chopped asparagus or broccoli
- 1 T lemon juice
- 2 T olive oil
- 1/3 cup grated cheese of your choosing (parmesan works well)

Sauté bacon pieces. Cook vegetables in boiling water 3 or 4 minutes until tender. Remove with slotted spoon and add fettuccine to the boiling water and cook according to directions on the package. Drain pasta and return to pot. Add bacon, vegetable, lemon juice, and olive oil to pot and gently toss. Serve on a plate and sprinkle with grated cheese.

Baked Fish with Tomatoes

Ingredients to serve one—double the amounts to serve two:

½ pound fillet, skinned and de-boned (your choice of fish)
3 T extra-virgin olive oil
2 T lemon juice
2 T chopped basil leaves
Dash each of salt and pepper
1 medium tomato, topped and sliced (about ¼ inch thick)
3 T grated cheese of your choosing (parmesan works well)

Combine olive oil, lemon juice, salt, and pepper and cover the bottom of a flat baking dish with the mixture.

Place fillets on mixture and then turn them over. Top with basil, tomato slices, and lastly, the grated cheese.

Bake in a preheated 400 degree oven for 10 minutes or until large end of the fillets flakes easily.

Cheesy Perch

You can also use other freshwater fish fillets. Ingredients to serve one—double the amounts to serve two:

½ pound perch fillets
½ cup cheesy cracker crumbs (like Cheez-its or other cheese-flavored crackers)
1/3 cup flour
1 egg
1 cup water
Dash each of salt and pepper
½ cup extra-virgin olive oil

Make fine crumbs of the crackers, either with a rolling pin or a food processor.

Combine the flour and cracker crumbs.

Using a fork, beat the egg, salt, and pepper into the water.

Dip each fillet into the water-egg mixture and sauté on both sides in the olive oil in a preheated nonstick skillet.

Fish Patties

Ingredients to serve one—double the amounts to serve two:

Chop two cups of flaked, boneless fish, either raw or cooked. Almost any kind of fish works just fine. A great way to use leftovers. Combine the chopped fish with:

1 egg
½ chopped onion
Dash each of salt and pepper (preferably lemon pepper)
2 T chopped green or red pepper

Add 1 cup of water to 1 cup complete pancake mix until it is the consistency you use for pancakes. Add the batter to the fish and other ingredients until it has the consistency of potato salad. Drop two large spoonfuls on a hot, greased grill or nonstick frying pan, forming patties. Fry until well browned on both sides.

This sounds like a lot of food for one person and it is, but if this is the only thing you eat for a meal (and I have done it many times), it will disappear.

Salmon Patties for Two*

Ingredients to serve two:

1 cup mashed potatoes (with milk and butter)
1-6 oz. can salmon, drained, skin, and bones removed
¼ cup chopped onion
3 saltine crackers, crushed
1/8 t salt and pepper
1 egg, separated
2 T vegetable oil

In medium bowl, combine the potatoes, salmon, onion, cracker crumbs, and egg yolk; mix well. Beat egg white until stiff.

Courtesy Judy Jenkins, Staples, MN

Macaroni and Cheese for Two*

Ingredients to serve two:

1½ cups cooked elbow macaroni
1 cup (4 oz.) shredded sharp cheese
½ cup milk
1 egg, lightly beaten
½ t salt
1 T butter or margarine

In medium bowl, combine the macaroni, cheese, milk, egg, and salt. Mix well.

Pour into a greased 1 qt. shallow baking dish. Dot with butter; bake uncovered at 350 degrees for 30 minutes.

*Courtesy Judy Jenkins, Staples, MN

CHAPTER 8
Desserts

Strawberry-Rhubarb Dessert

Ingredients to serve one—double the amounts to serve two:

 1 cup early rhubarb, cut into ½-inch chunks
 1 cup fresh strawberries (wild if available)
 1 t vanilla
 4 T sugar
 ½ cup water

Place all ingredients in a pot and simmer 10 minutes or until rhubarb is tender.

Sauce Made from Dried Fruit

Ingredients to serve one—double the amounts to serve two:

> 2 cups dried fruit (dried apricots, prunes, pineapple, and apple all work well)
> Water, enough to cover
> ½ cup sugar
> 1 t lemon juice
> Lemon or orange peel

Cover fruit with water and let stand overnight. Add sugar and lemon juice and let simmer 30 minutes or until fruit is soft. Serve hot or cold. Add citrus peel for garnish.

Pineapple–Peach Salsa

Ingredients to serve one—double the amounts to serve two:

 1 small can crushed pineapple
 1 peach, pitted, peeled, and chopped
 2 T green chili pepper, chopped
 ½ t ground ginger

Combine all ingredients thoroughly (including pineapple juice). Refrigerate, covered.

Cherry Salsa

Ingredients to serve one—double the amounts to serve two:

 1 cup cherry jam
 3 T minced onion
 3 T minced green pepper
 3 T chopped chilies
 6 drops Tabasco sauce

Combine all ingredients thoroughly.

Rice Pudding

Ingredients to serve one—double the amounts to serve two:

1 cup cooked rice (regular or wild rice)
1/3 cup raisins
1/3 cup sugar
½ cup milk
2 T cinnamon
1 t vanilla

Combine all ingredients and serve hot or cold

Wild Rice with Wild Berries

Ingredients to serve one—double the amounts to serve two:

1 cup cooked wild rice
1 cup wild berries such as blue berries, raspberries, strawberries, etc.
4 T whipped cream

Combine rice and berries and top with whipped cream. Rice may be hot or cold.

Orange Cranberry Bars*

Ingredients to make 8 bars:

¼ cup all-purpose flour
1½ t sugar
2 T cold butter
2 T chopped nuts of your choosing

Topping:
2 T beaten egg
1½ t milk
¾ t grated orange peel
¼ t vanilla extract
1/3 cup sugar
1½ t all-purpose flour
¼ cup fresh or frozen cranberries
2 T flaked coconut
2 T chopped pecans

In a bowl, combine flour and sugar; cut in butter until mixture resembles coarse crumbs. Stir in pecans. Press into an 8x4x2 inch loaf pan coated with nonstick cooking spray. Bake at 350 degrees for 15 minutes.

Meanwhile, in a bowl, combine the egg, milk, orange peel, and vanilla. Combine sugar and flour, gradually add to egg mixture and mix well. Fold in the cranberries, coconut, and pecans. Spread over crust. Bake 15–20 minutes or until golden brown.

Courtesy Betsy Hayenga, Waite Park, MN

The Perfect Dessert for Salmon*

If you grill or broil a fillet of salmon for a special meal, the ideal dessert is a dish of praline ice cream covered with a jigger of Kahlua liqueur.

Courtesy Kristy Wilger, Royalton, MN

Other Cookbooks by Dr. Lund

101 Favorite Freshwater Fish Recipes

Gourmet Freshwater Fish Recipes

101 Favorite Wild Rice Recipes

150 Ways to Enjoy Potatoes

Camp Cooking, Made Easy and Fun

Cooking Minnesotan

The Soup Cookbook

The Scandinavian Cookbook

German Home Cooking

Italian Home Cooking

Eating Green and Loving It